FAMILY KILLS

LARON SPALDING

Family Kills
Copyright © 2022 by Laron Spalding

Tellwell Talent
www.tellwell.ca

ISBN
978-0-2288-8023-3 (Hardcover)
978-0-2288-8022-6 (Paperback)
978-0-2288-8024-0 (eBook)

April 15, 2014 when I was 42 is the date my life changed forever … and for the better I pray! Within my own family, Jesus stepped in and accomplished victory over death for me, and now I am living this new life to the fullest.

I had no idea that the enemy watched me as I cooked for society every day at the food truck business I owned and operated in Louisville, Kentucky. At my truck, I served the finest of foods. But having overlooked the lessons that God meant for me to learn, I took life for granted, and I hired the enemy, sexed the enemy, and played with the enemy to my loss.

My sister-in-law and I worshipped together in the same church—and committed sin together; however, I did not think this would make the enemy try to kill me! This woman is married to one of my brothers. I loved and protected this woman like she was my very own sister, because she is my niece's mother. She became near to my heart over the years, and there was nothing she could do that I would not forgive.

One day while looking out my bedroom window, I heard a voice saying, "I'm going to get you when you come outside."

I replied, "I don't do anything to anyone but grill!" But it was no accident that I was hit by my sister-in-law's vehicle and dragged a half a mile down the road.

I lay still and cold behind a nightclub until the ambulance came to get my nearly lifeless body. Upon arriving at the hospital, I didn't awake for 30 days. I lay breathless, and in a coma with my body hooked up to breathing machines. Upon awakening, I saw my other sister-in-law standing in my room. I had no idea what had taken place because I had no memories of the accident. I was just in the present, at this one point in my life.

After a month or so I began to realize that I was missing my right ear, my right nipple was gone, and I could barely talk or see because I had a traumatic brain injury (TBI) and a tracheostomy (breathing tube) in my throat. My upper left side had been mangled; my ribs were fractured, and amputation of my left arm was pending. Further, my would-be killer (my sister-in-law and former lover) remained on the loose.

By God's grace, I received mercy—and today I find myself living a new life as a disciple of Jesus Christ! Once, I thought I accomplished everything on my own, but God blessed me to understand and believe that He is the one who has my best interests in His hands!

My story is worth sharing with others. This journey has been long and through God, I have found myself being an inspiration to all who assisted Him in helping get me well. Whether you are a believer or not, and whether you are living or resting in peace, every day above ground is an opportunity to get it right with God because going to hell makes no sense! God is the amazing creator of everything!

Before that accident, for three years straight, I served Louisville, Kentucky, with the finest of foods; after the accident, I woke up in the hospital wrapped up from head to toe like a new prize after being dragged, and nearly killed, by my sister-in-law in her vehicle. As I rested, healed, and waited on God to bless me with life again, the doctors God blessed to work on my body got to the point of giving up. They thought I was going to die.

Thank God my true loved ones stepped in! First, my brother and nephew made vital decisions regarding my surgeries. They also changed my bandages when hospital staff did not have time to tend to me. However, I was still not doing well, and so medical staff contacted my family to give them the bad news. Upon notifying my family that I was not going to make it, they learned I had a daughter, and that she was in charge of all decisions regarding my life.

When my daughter was told that her dad was not going to make it, it was recommended that she pull plug on me. She called her grandmother (her mother's mother) for advice, and her granny replied, "That is your daddy, baby. Do what you feel is right." My daughter then told the doctors that her daddy was going to live, and so the doctors had no choice but to wait and see if I did!

My situation was precarious. Because of how damaged my body was, the staff were on high alert. Most gave up on me, but not my mother. Mama said to God, "No, not my son!" My mother spent every day and night in the hospital, walking back and forth talking to God, making her request known until He answered her! Some people who visited were just playing roles, pretending they really cared for me, but they didn't pray for me. But others, like my mother, really cared. She stayed in prayer with God constantly. I thank God that He hears what we say and knows our hearts.

The enemy was present every day that I lay resting in that coma, and each person who came to visit my motionless body had to sign in and surrender their phones. People were worried, but no crying was tolerated; those who believed I was going to die had no idea that I was just on vacation, resting. I had worked hard for three years, and I believe that God wanted to give me a chance to rest during that 30 days of coma. God favored me because I grilled for people in Jefferson County every day for three years, just to see customers smile at the goodness of the food. No doubt the devil meant what happened to me for evil, but God meant it for good!

Upon getting out of the hospital, God blessed me to believe with all my heart that revenge was HIS! My sister-in-law—who hit me and dragged me a half a mile down the street before the car released my clothing—returned to my apartment to rob me, unaware that she would meet one of my brothers there. Upon telling him what she had done to me, he beat her ass! Unfortunately, the devil would later use this as an excuse to free her from prosecution for her crime. She told her attorney, and her husband (another one of my brothers), that I beat her up, which is why she ran me over. The court system allowed her to make a deal for two years, with credit for time served. She told this lie continuously to her husband during her 15 months in jail—which she spent fighting the case!

Today, I forgive her, and I am constantly thankful for the opportunity to live life again. I remain steadfastly focused on the lessons the Lord has taught me. I feel like I have overcome the temptations of the world. I no longer look at things as I once did, nor do I view things as accidental; instead, every day is an opportunity to display how great God is!

Upon release from the hospital, though not yet completely healed, I *thought* I was okay, and I went forward after my accident without God's protection. My life quickly fell apart. My food trailer was destroyed, my truck was stolen, my clothes disappeared, I became addicted to drugs and before long I was homeless! I was striving to get well and overcome the devil's attempt to kill me, but I had missed the lessons God wanted to teach me.

One lesson God wanted to teach me was about money. When this journey began, I had already accepted that money is not everything (though it has its place); but due to the lessons God taught me through my accident, I now see money as an opportunity to display how responsible I am as a steward of gifts from the MOST HIGH in fact, I yearn for the opportunity to help the needy and less fortunate so that I live with God always, in peace.

This is what happened. Upon release from the hospital, I visited an attorney my brother had found for me while I was in a coma. At that time, not only did I have to walk with a walker, but my brain injury was so severe that I didn't know what was going on; however, I was convinced that I was on my way to seek justice, and I believed God had me. The attorney stated that the insurance had lapsed, and that it was impossible to be successful in court because of how the justice system would handle this type of case. I had no understanding at this point that the criminal proceedings were not yet finalized, and that the attorney was chasing greed; all I knew was that my brother's connection fee was at stake … and, as I said, I believed God had me. I was on a great mission, even though I couldn't hear well, I was tired all the time, and I was really just a baby in a grown man's body.

Four months later, my now-ex-girlfriend and I visited this same attorney's office, and they offered me $30,000 dollars! I accepted the offer and left the bank with $30,000 in my hand … but I did not realize that I was with the enemy! Upon opening a bank account, I was not well enough to understand that it would not be wise to put her name on my account. What a BIG mistake! During my recuperation, my ex-girlfriend withdrew $10,000 dollars from my account. Because I was injured and healing from my TBI, and because I was staying in her home and needed her, I did not say anything to anyone about this until this moment.

The next thing that happened was, because I love my daughter to the fullest, I gave her spending money as well as $1,000 for her first apartment. She told her mother about the insurance settlement, and, in turn, her mother went to the child maintenance program and told them about my settlement and they pulled $6,500 out of my bank account!

At this time, I felt very taken advantage of; it was as if God was taking me through the 'do's and don'ts' of life and teaching me that truly, the love of money is the root of all evil.

When I moved out of my ex-girlfriend's place, things did not go well. From someone who used to visit me in the hospital very day, hearing and listening to concerns about me, she became a person who I had to get an emergency protection order (EPO) against! Ultimately, within the first year after waking up from the coma, I moved to seven different places, no matter if it was family members I was living with, or companies that specialized in housing those with brain injuries, $500 was the number everyone wanted for rent.

First, I tried living with family, but because everything was new to me, this did not work. I was like a newborn trying to run. I was unable to think and comprehend.

Then I tried living at a brain injury facility; however, the housing company I rented from had limited capability for services such as washing clothes and bathing, so I had to do that myself. On top of that, I didn't like what the hired staff cooked and so most of the time I ate cold cuts because I was not well enough to cook for myself. I entered four different brain injury companies. I did not last long with the brain injury programs because I wanted my independence back badly.

This was a challenging time And the devil's voice inside my head was strong. One time I heard it trying to inspire me to kill myself. I was sitting in the living room of a home where I was renting a room, and I heard the voice as clear as anything. I called the police, and they responded as soon as I explained the situation. They took me to a state hospital where I was evaluated for seven days and released. But I refused to give up and allow the devil to win; instead, my relationship with Jesus grew as never before, and I began to dream about forgiving the enemy for what she had done. I knew in my heart that this was the only way I could heal … from the inside out.

And so I carry on with my healing and I cling to God, who is answering my prayers. As part of my physical recovery,

I regularly visit a brain injury doctor. Slowly, I am getting better. Today, a home nurse visited me to change the bandages where my ear used to be (my right ear came off when the car dragged my face on the concrete). A new ear has been placed inside my right arm to get used to my body, and it will be attached to my head in time. This is not easy to bear; pain often either wakes me up or prevents me from going to sleep, and there have been times when I was intimidated by the pain. However, I truly believe in 'no pain, no gain'!

Every now and then I visit the brain injury companies and speak with others who are suffering as I have. I like sharing good news about what I can do today, versus what I couldn't do yesterday and so I share with them what God has brought me through. This keeps me humble and grateful. God has blessed my healing to a point where I am well enough to discover opportunities for fellowship.

The things I am experiencing right now are the most difficult changes I have had to face in my entire life, but I know it's important to keep a good attitude. I don't allow what is going on with me to influence my behavior going forward. I have accepted what has happened—but what is *going* to happen will occur by faith, not attitude! I make sure to show my appreciation to God for every bit of assistance He has blessed me to receive during my recovery process, and though I continue to live with disabilities, I realize how blessed I am to be breathing.

I have learned so much. I have been forced to move at a slower pace now, and that has made me grateful for everything I am blessed to do. I have learned that the evil one will do anything to pull me down, speed me up or try to delay God's blessings for me … but no evil weapon formed against me shall prosper! This new life of mine is filled with challenges that, with the help of Jesus, I am destined to overcome. An example is when my sister-in-law tried to 'friend' me on social media; I forgive her … but I don't want to see her anymore in this lifetime! So I rejected her request. It would be giving the devil another opportunity to try to destroy my life!

Because of my faith in God, I now make wiser decisions and I have learned to trust God with everything. He has answered me time and time again. My brain injury no longer has a strong hold on my 'do's and don'ts', and I realize that I must be prepared, and 'prayed up', for the unseen to be relevant. I also realize that I must not give up or lose my faith. Change is a must, because the old person I used to be would never have imagined that the enemy was within my own family and had grown so close to me!

Jealousy, driven by the devil, reached its fullness. Merciful God saved me from my sister-in-law's failed attempt on my life. How happy and excited I am to know that only God is the true judge, and not man, because my sister-in-law has been deemed by the law to be disabled and mentally challenged and allowed to return to society. But I know that God knows her heart, just as He knows mine and everyone else's.

Looking back, I know I participated in foolishness with the enemy, and by doing so I welcomed the devil into my home. I was the lease holder, but the devil wanted to take over. My family member was tricked by the devil into believing she could ensure my demise, that she could change God's plan for my life. However, because God lives, I have life today. His blood is the reason no evil weapon formed against me will damage me. As long as I stand with Jesus, she can't touch me.

I did not even know what had happened until my brain began to heal. Though I was a grown man, when I was broken by that car I became a baby again, unknowing and unable to care for myself. Today, however, I have been blessed with a new life and all things are new. God had me then, and He's got me now.

At the beginning of my healing, I had no control of the times that I slept; it was if I was sleeping my life away! For months my eyes barely opened and, when they did, my vision was badly blurred. I recall an associate's wife saying, "Look, his eyes are open!" as if my brown eyes were a surprise to see!

My getting well took prayer from people around the world, as well as significant effort on my part to *want* to be well. At first, I couldn't even walk up and down steps without holding onto the rails. It was as if my legs were broken I had no strength and no balance. Walking the treadmill and running in the swimming pool made my balance much better, but the most important thing for my healing was to let go and let God. As I did, I began to heal!

There have been times I chose to move without God's protective hand … and I always paid the price, with a lot of regrets! Then I go back to God. I could not talk, write, or count, but my faith in Jesus kept me believing that I would overcome the devil's plan to kill me. I awoke from the coma weighing only 160 pounds and my weight goes up and down as I heal … but as long as I stay positive, I am winning! Making progress is my mission.

One thing I learned is that I needed to become independent, and so I have turned down many offers of assistance because I know that I must learn to look after myself if I want to get better. I can't depend on others all the time. I need to depend on God first, and myself second, and so I have distanced myself. This has helped me really focus on what God wants for me. I have started to remember dreams I had while I was in the coma, and I am working on fulfilling those dreams. I know what God has in store for me is good but letting go of people and things of old is part of it. I accept that every day will be a struggle, but because I believe I can do all things in Christ Jesus, I am strengthened. I will always be in recovery from this tragedy, but by His grace I now live a more productive life.

Further, I realize I must position myself to hear from the HIGHEST every day. With Him, I find myself overcoming what hindered me yesterday. I have learned to appreciate the smallest of things that I once took for granted; like nails, rails and—most importantly—common sense. I know I must be prepared spiritually and mentally in everything I do and say, because my words are 'into existence', so my thinking must be fresh every day.

I have fully accepted God's plans for my life because He answered my prayers and accepted my supplication. God a fight with my sister-in-law would cause me to put her out of my apartment. God also knew that I had enough love for her to change my mind—which would reveal His Plans for us both. God knew that I needed rest, and He also knew how to accomplish this. The road to recovery has been long, and the people God has brought into my life to assist Him with my recovery, and to ensure His HIS healing takes place, are amazing.

For a long time I could not remember anything about the accident, but as I gave up the old person that I used to be and accepted the newness of me, healing began, and I started to recall things. I had to learn to forgive, and to do this I began to focus on the things I used to talk to God about before my injuries. Then, I often talked to God about what I would be like as an old man. I started doing that again, and guess what? I realized that every day I'm blessed just to be able to breathe. Now, I fully understand that I'm not promised tomorrow, and I must live like today is my last day! Now, I have a different understanding of things—and of God—and so I am not quick to do just anything that enters my thoughts. The pride I once lived with is no longer, because God has blessed me with His amazing grace!

I woke up not knowing what had happened to me, or what I had been through, but knowing that I believed in God and that Jesus had helped me make it through everything. While I was in a coma, I saw myself in the front of the courthouse, talking to God. I understood that He was showing me I was going to have encounters with thieves and make bad decisions warranting a judge's intervention. God showed me truth, but I have come through that now, and my God deserves every second that I'm blessed to breathe!

Before my injuries I lived in at the corner of 26th and Chestnut, an area where people, including police officers, were being killed at an alarming rate. It was if this corner was the devil's playground! I believed God was looking after me, and that no weapon formed against me would prosper, but I also harmed myself by getting high, feeding the Holy Spirit poison. I wasn't willing to give God 100 percent.

After my injuries, I understood that God doesn't settle for 'lukewarm'. God wants all or nothing. Now, I have given it all to Jesus, and I find myself living in peace and serenity. I live in Christ, and I can do all things through Christ who strengthens me.

That morning when I heard the enemy say, "I am going to get you," as I looked out my bedroom window, I naively thought, "I don't do anything to anyone but grill!" and I was not afraid; however, a few days later I thought I was saying my final goodbyes on Earth. Little did I know I was about to transformed into the new person I am today!

I know I will continue to have difficulties in some areas of my life, but I maintain a good attitude and believe myself to be a winner. Before God's grace changed my life, it seemed like no matter where I went, or what I did, the devil was always there. In every area my life, everything was a struggle. Now, I have accepted that I am blessed to live this new life, that it is part of God's plan, and the devil is gone.

But even with all my blessings, because of my brain injury, life can seem like a blur. When that happens there are two things I try. First, I pray for understanding and acceptance of my purpose in this new life; and second, I reach backwards for tools and talents that once helped me achieve things, like the self-assurance and confidence the devil tried steal. I always find that prayer is more effective.

Before my injuries, I often welcomed family members over to my apartment at all hours of the night, for unwholesome purposes. Now that I have a new lease on life, I feel like the devil used my unrighteous behavior against me. At church we believe that we 'are not saved to sit, but to serve'. I was very selfish in my past life, and I did not serve. I attended classes to prove that I was willing to serve … and then I stopped attending them to drink beer, along with other foolishness.

My sister-in-law and I were both on this path, and that's how the attempted murder happened. Easter Sunday was approaching, and she and I were starting to get high together more and more often. But despite our sinful behavior, how could I have imagined that in only a few short days, she would try to steal my life away from me?

The devil inspired my sister-in-law to hit me with her vehicle and drag me down the street, and then return to my apartment to rob me as I lay half-dead in an alley behind a nightclub. When she returned to my apartment, she was met by my other brother. She told him what she'd done and he beat her ass! Unfortunately, the devil used this to free my sister-in-law from justice. She told her husband, my brother, that I beat her up and that's why she ran me over me. He borrowed money to pay an attorney so the attorney could present this lie to the courts. It got her a light sentence but changed my life forever. My sister-in-law received a two-year sentence with credit for time served—for trying to kill me!

I realize the battle is not mine, but the Lord's. I am apart of God's plan, and I truly believe that my new life is a blessed one to live. I am in and out of surgery, and I am faced with daily obstacles that challenge my abilities to remember and remain focused, but I have a duty to be obedient and pay close attention to all instructions set forth by God, through my doctors. I must ensure that I become all that the Lord has predestined me to become. God is the director of my footsteps. Without God, I would either be in the graveyard, my death unsolved, or I would not be able to live on my own and I would be dependent on the system for the rest of my life!

I have gotten better every day since my injuries occurred. I even became acquainted with the guy who is sleeping with my ex-girlfriend. It was upsetting, but with the grace of God I remained calm. The 'old me' would have challenged this man, but the new me did not. God has taught me that the smoothest approach to conflict goes the furthest, protecting me. This is a blessing because physically, I am unable to sustain further injuries.

Before my sister-in-law's attack, I owned a barbecue business. After the attack, while still badly injured, I refused to sit still and wait on God to finish healing me. Instead, I fixed up my food trailer very nicely, preparing to do business upon getting well. Then, upon going into surgery to have a nerve removed from the right side of my ankle and put into the right side of my face (because I could not smile equally), the evil one destroyed my truck. The owner of a brain injury program I was in asked if I was interested in selling my truck. I replied, 'no,' because I have never sold anything that God has blessed me with … but then my truck was stolen.

It was a blow, but I learned to take the bitter with the sweet. Nothing mattered if I was not well, and so I kept my attitude in check. God showed me that my job was to keep striving to get well. I had allowed the enemy in by not 'letting go and letting God'.

There were more tests for me. As I struggled to cope with living independently, two of my brothers who I loved deeply were killed, but because a former employee had pushed me down a flight of stairs I was unable to attend their funerals. Next, another former employee asked me to join a female and him in having sex. Knowing that he had AIDS, I replied, "I've never done that, and I am not going to start at this point!" I had to accept that the devil still wanted me dead and it was my responsibility to not give him the satisfaction!

When I was finally well enough to hold a job, I entered a cooking program to relearn the skills that I once knew, and to prove to myself that I was worthy of being a business owner. Upon taking my final exam, I was approached by a student who had graduated already. She had gotten a job at a famous restaurant, and she asked me if I wanted a job. I replied, "Yes," and began working at that restaurant throughout the Christmas holiday season. Surely, God had begun to open the windows of Heaven and pour out a blessing on me!

The next thing that happened is that I received my own apartment through a government program I'd applied to years before. At the time I applied, I was told nothing was in place to bump my name up on the list, despite my injuries and what I had suffered, but a brain injury program worker helped me get the place.

Since then, God's blessings have come rolling down, and it hasn't stopped! But because Satan seeks to steal, kill, and destroy, he's always putting challenges in my way. In this case, the company I rented the apartment from sold the apartment, but didn't pay the water bill first, and so the water was shut off. But God told me that wisdom is better than strength, and to be patient. He gave me patience from Heaven and my water was restored.

Satan challenged me again, this time at my job. I began expressing my blessings to other employees at the famous restaurant I was working at … and they fired me! Months later, I was notified that I should seek an attorney because of how I was fired by this restaurant, and that I should sue for civil violations. Instead, I filed a complaint with the Human Rights Commission, which was less troublesome for the restaurant, because I was at a point where it was time to show compassion. God rewarded me with just enough financial compensation to get a used washer and a dryer for my apartment, which I really needed. I am sure God blessed me to get the desires of my heart because I showed compassion to this company!

My hospital stay started on April 20, 2011, and I stayed in the intensive care unit the whole time. When I was first in the hospital and unconscious, I was labeled as 'John Doe' for several days because my family had no knowledge of the attempt on my life. They only found out because my niece's friend lived a couple of doors from me and told my niece what had happened to me. That's how my brother got information about me. He rushed to the hospital and became my decision-maker until my daughter took over! When my brother got to the University Hospital, this is what they told him about my condition:

- The MRI of my brain indicated hypoperfusion (decreased blood flow) in the supraorbital (above the orbit of the eye) area and right parietal lobe.

- While the ventricles (chambers of the brain that contain fluid) and sulci (brain tissue) were appropriate for my age, the MRI suggested that my brain air cells were filled with fluids and were injured.
- There was enhancement and mucosal thickening of the left maxillary and spheroid sinuses with associated air fluid levels.

God has been trying to get my attention for a long time and has been with me through some very trying moments over the course of my life. In the past, I have been hit by a car, and suffered a concussion. I have also been shot in the back of my head and in both of my legs. I recovered from these situations and was more careful about my actions, and who I could trust. But I considered my sister-in-law to be family, and so I never thought for a moment that my blood would be on *her* hands. I never took precautionary measures when it came to her! But after the devil moved her to try to kill me, I have learned that what the devil meant for evil, God meant for good! So how amazing is God? Let's witness together!

My hospital records note that surgery was needed to save my life. Doctors were instructed to be present for all proceedings and I was admitted to trauma services because:

- I needed a skin a replacement to the right side of my face, due to facial injuries.
- My left arm needed to be amputated because it had been mangled.
- My ribs were fractured.

- I had head trauma on the GCS (Glasgow Coma Scale, a tool for assessing consciousness in patients with TBI) I was between 5 and 6.
- I needed intubation.

I was unable to be intubated until I was presented to the trauma bay. I was heavily sedated at this time and even though I had injuries to my right shoulder, chest, and abdominal area, I never felt any pain throughout it all!

Below describes the medical steps that were done before I was taken to the operating room, as well as some of the post-surgery steps:

- A timeout was performed to verify that I was the correct patient, at the correct site, and that the correct procedures were being performed.
- I was laid supine on the operating table and general endotracheal anesthesia was induced.
- Granulation tissue (the primary type of tissue that will fill in a wound that is healing by secondary intention) was irrigated.
- Debridement (surgical removal of damaged tissue) was performed on my complex right facial avulsion (forcible detachment, in this case my ear) bringing the site of the injury into a state of healthy, bleeding tissue.
- My head injury and jaw injury were treated: The tempos parietal lobe (of my brain) was exposed, and my lower jaw was shattered.

My file said:

This patient is well known to our services. He has a traumatic scalp avulsion and ear avulsion, and an open wound with exposed calvarium. This was grossly contaminated and required multiple debridement. Once this was complete, the abdomen was irrigated with several liters of warm, normal saline. The fascia then was closed with 2-0 looped PDS sutures. Elective skin was left open due to gross contamination from the compounded injuries. Incisions were packed with saline soaked kerlix and covered with ABD (high absorbency sterile pads) and tape. Patient was transferred to recovery in critical condition. Doctors were present for all portions of this procedure. The patient was prepped for a different surgery by the plastic team because his right ear and right nipple were removed by the dragging; patient's right hand has injuries that need attention.

When the surgeries were over, my wounds were dressed in a 50/50 solution of betadine and peroxide, and I was taken to the burn unit for stabilization. I could not breathe without a tracheostomy and a ventilator. Being unconscious, and having no control of anything, I was constantly talking to the Almighty. I often visualized myself in front of the courthouse, where in the past I'd had many troubles. Not many things had gone my way in this courthouse, and so I took this vision as God's way of warning me that more troubles would come my way before my dreams would come true unlike anything I could have ever imagined!

I know hospital staff did for me what God called them to do. They treated my severe acidosis as best they could, while prepping me for the surgeries I needed. They performed oral and maxillofacial (OMFS) surgery on my damaged jaw and skull. They also did an exploratory laparotomy (incision in the abdominal wall to gain access to the abdominal cavity) to determine what abdominal injuries I had. They did X-rays of my right hand because I had open wounds over the second, third and fourth joints. And, of course, they amputated my left arm. They did the arm amputation on my left, and the hand surgery on my right, concurrently. My brother, who was acting for me at the time, consented to the amputation.

The medical notes regarding the amputation are as follows:

> *The patient was brought to the operating room and was placed on the operating table in supine position with left upper extremity extended out. Preoperative antibiotics were given. Time was performed. The patient's left upper extremity was prepped and draped in a sterile fashion. The tourniquet was removed prior to prepping the extremity. The left upper extremity was examined. The distal portion of the humerus was missing. The elbow joint was completely destroyed and unstable. This extensive soft tissue, muscle, tendon and nerve loss to the dorsal aspect extended from the proximal*

third of the humerus to the distal third of the forearm, as well as to roughly two-thirds of the volar aspect of the forearm. Given the magnitude and severity of the soft tissue and bony destruction, it was felt that attempting to save the extremity would worsen the patient's acidosis and endanger his life. Thus, we proceed with trans-humerus amputation with flaps in a fish-mouth fashion. An incision was made overlaying these flaps at the most distal area of healthy tissue. Dissection was carried down through the subcutaneous tissue using Bovie electrocautery (a surgical technique which uses high frequency current to remove unwanted tissue, cauterize blood vessels or make incisions). After the skin flaps had been reflected proximally, the biceps brachial artery and vein were identified, doubly migrated proximal and distal to the planned level of bony resection. The biceps brachial was divided. The radial, median and ulnar nerves were pulled dismally and transected, allowing to retract into the proximal musculature. The cephalic vein and basilic vein were doubly located and sutured with 3-0 silk. The lateral medial antebrachial cutaneous nerves, as well as the dorsal antebrachial cutaneous nerves were identified, pulled distally transected. The brachialis muscle, as well as the biceps brachia, were divided down to the level of the bone, using Bovie cautery. Dissection was carried around circumferentially through the triceps brachii down to the level of the humerus. The level of intended bone resection was marked, and the bone was hemostasis was checked and achieved. The wound was irrigated copiously. The bone was found to be smooth. The interior and posterior fascia over flexor and extensor muscle masses were brought together and closed with simple irruption Vicryl sutures. The deep dermal sutures were closed with Vicryl sutures. The skin was then closed with staples. Adaptic dry dressing, bacitracin and soft dressing were applied to the left transhumeral stump. Attention was then turned toward the patient's right dorsal (back of) hand, which was placed on an arm board. The right dorsal hand was prepped and draped in sterile fashion. There were wounds overlying the dorsal aspects of the right second, this and fourth metacarpal phalangeal joints. The wounds were irrigated copiously, and soft tissue was debrided, including exterior tendons overlying the second and this MCP joints. Overlying the fourth MCP joints, this was only skin loss. The wound was irrigated again. Adaptic dry dressing and a soft dressing was applied overlying the right dorsal hand. The patient tolerated the procedure. He remained in the operating room for exploratory laparotomy by General Surgery, thus including the portion of the case performed by Hand Surgery. Medications at time of consult.

1. *Aspirin*
2. *Dulcolax suppository*
3. *Chlorhexidine*
4. *Dakin's (1/8 strength)*
5. *Colace*
6. *Lovenox*
7. *Sliding scale insulin*
8. *Lansoprazole*
9. *Metronidazole*
10. *Milk of Magnesia*
11. *Potassium Chloride*
12. *Vancomycin*
13. *Dilaudid as needed for dressing changes.*

My medical reports also said:

> *The patient has a left transfemoral amputation that is wrapped in an Ace wrap. Enology diagnosis and comorbidities (multiple diseases) include:*

14. *Immobility syndrome secondary to multi trauma*
15. *Avulsion of the right face*
16. *Left transhumeral amputation*
17. *Traumatic brain injury*
18. *Right hand wound*
19. *Road rash to chest and abdomen*
20. *Jejunal (small intestine) injury*
21. *Rib fracture.*
22. *Pulmonary contusion.*

23. *Respiratory failure post tracheostomy*
24. *Leukocytosis (high white blood cell count)*

The doctor wrote:

> *At this time, I feel the patient will likely be a candidate for acute inpatient rehabilitation program once his mental status improves and he is more able to participate in therapies. He would be a good candidate for the brain injury problem as well, but again, we will continue to follow him to make sure that he does have some improvement functionally where he is able to participate.*

I did well to that point in my recovery. However, after my surgery doctors found a large blood mass on my back. Initially, medical staff thought it was a hematoma (a collection of blood outside of blood vessels) but needle placement demonstrated it was a return of bleeding. I was taken to the operation room once again to evacuate the blood. I tolerated the procedure well, there were no complications, and I was taken to the post-operative care unit in stable condition.

It is apparent that black lives *do* matter … at least to God. My hospital bills were at least a million dollars, but God said that no evil weapon formed against me shall prosper. I was struggling to live, and breathing only with the assistance of medical intervention, but I continued to fight the good fight set before me!

Surely, I am a sinner saved by grace. I haven't always made the wisest choices in life, but today I pray about all things because I need God's assurance and protection always. I never realized how much my life was in God's hands until the devil tried to steal it away from me and I was unable to defend myself. I attempt to hear His holy voice every day that I am blessed to be awake to witness!

I still have my share of challenges, but I have gone from not being able to think, and unable to do the simplest things mentally or physically to being thankful for what I can do today, like attend church services online, serve society with the finest of foods, and drive a car. I have accepted this new life, with fresh desires and ideas, and I have been living a life of recovery for seven years. I go forward at a pace that, at first, only made sense to the Holy Spirit because it is so slow … but I walk with faith throughout this healing process, and I believe I can do all things in Christ Jesus' name. By God's grace, I am no longer mentally and physically in despair and disrepair. Amen.

Being humble is a state of mind. I only understand now what being humble means because God has blessed me to live a peaceful life, unlike the way I lived before. Before, I made bad choices! Today, I truly trust God because He said that the battle is HIS. I have had my share of turning the other cheek, but today I always make sure I pray about the situation to my Heavenly Father at prayer time, because I know God will guide me on the right path.

It's taken me a long time, but now I am content and patient like never before. I have had my share of difficulties since my injuries—mostly caused by trying to rush my healing progress—but I have forgiven my sister-in-law's evil attempt on my life. I had to, because if I did not, I would be stuck in that same state of mind that I was in before and I would not have allowed God to heal to me as he has.

Today, I am humbly grateful because God has blessed me to live again! I refuse to accept any of the glory for the breath that I breathe today because the truth is, I was on the devil's path before that terrible day, and I did not listen to God's attempts to help me have a better life. I thought I knew it all. I got in my own way and I guess I needed my sister-in-law's assistance to get out of it. It is not something I could have done on my own. As I've said … what the enemy meant for evil, God meant for good. I truly believe that I have no limitations.

I am missing my left arm, but I am right-handed, so that is a blessing. Sure, it takes more time to do things with only one hand, but it makes me slow down and focus. I have much to be grateful for. I still have my mind, body, and soul! Medical miracles abound in my life. When I was in a coma and in the hospital, all my blood was drawn out of my body, filtered by a machine, and put back in my body so I could live. Today, I went to the prosthetic clinic to get my prosthetic arm worked on, and to pick up my charger for the arm. My left hand opens and closes like a normal hand. If that's not a blessing from God, I don't know what is.

Another blessing I am grateful for is that, thanks to God, I have learned tolerance and how to hold my tongue, both things I didn't have before. Recently my neighbor approached me and said that her daughter had seen me chastising my dog, and if I did it again, she was going to call the law and get my dog taken away. Though I was thinking, *mind your business*, I smiled and kept silent. I do not mistreat my dog; I am blessed to be raising the world's smartest dog, and I would never do that. Eventually the woman left me alone, and there was no problem. If I had told her to mind her own business, it would have created trouble, but I did not because I trust God to guide me. I know now that if I take one step, God will take two.

As I continued to heal and get better, I asked in prayer for God to put me in a position to help someone. I reached out to a recovery hospital and met a woman named Tiffany. She had lost her brother and had begun to drink uncontrollably. I started her on her way to recovery. One test I had with her is that her neighbor pushed her down and she asked if I could respond. I didn't respond right away because I needed God's guidance. I didn't want things to go badly. Eventually the police were called!

I can't trust myself to read situations correctly with a TBI, and that is why I must rely so heavily on God. Once, my neighbor called and asked me if I wanted to barbecue with them. I said yes, because I create my own barbecue sauce and it is very good. I wanted to share it.

At the barbecue, one female guest (another neighbor) had anger on her heart because her sister had stolen my cellphone and I reported the theft to the police. She was angry at me for that, and she began to verbally attack me, telling me that I could not grill even though at one point in my life I made my living as a grill expert. Eventually, she became so nasty that I left the barbecue and said good night.

Things were not over between us, however, because later she came to my apartment and asked for forgiveness … and I said yes. However, I know that the devil leads a lot of folks to believing they can take advantage of my condition and so, while I sought to forgive her whole heartedly, I felt that she was up to something bad and so I was cautious around her.

I was right; she attempted to use me. As I was on my way to the store, I passed by her apartment, where she stood on her porch, talking on the phone. I asked her if she could help me tie one of my tennis shoes, as that is difficult for me. She said, "People are going to think I am your woman!" but I could tell that she said this just to make whoever was on the phone jealous.

The next day, I was sitting on her porch while she was not home (which I had done many times), resting with my dog and typing. She pulled in and said that she doesn't want me sitting on her porch anymore! She and I had been planning to grill for neighbors across the street from our apartments. I'd even gone to the store and bought all the ingredients to make the people happy and satisfied; but, after she said that to me, I quietly cancelled everything because I did not understand why she was acting like that.

I am highly grateful to be alive and positive minded, but tests like that to check my abilities keep coming … like when the hired recovery helper stole $20 out of my bedroom when making up my bed! I never complained about it because of the joy I felt at being alive. Such happiness cannot be expressed! Twenty dollars is nothing compared to that.

Despite my struggles, I am in a state of grace, and every day I am grateful for the lessons I have been taught, and to the teachers God has provided me with. For example, the brain injury specialists that God hired to accompany me while I was badly injured transported me back and forth to the college that I used to attend to take my reentry exams time and time again. They were patient with me, and they knew that for me to recover, failure was not an option!

I am also grateful for the way in which my body continues to heal. I jogged back and forth in the swimming pool the entire summer of 2016, and finally my balance has started to return. Walking on the treadmill also helped.

I am learning about how to look after myself. The chest pain I had yesterday was caused by an inflammation of the cartilage joining the ribs, called costochondritis. Costochondritis can be caused by emotional stress, and it can be painful but it's not dangerous. I learned that if I feel stress, I should try to identify the source of that stress and deal with it with regular exercise, muscle relaxation, mediation, or by simply taking time out.

Because I could not talk for quite some time when I first started healing, I listened to music, both when I was awake and when I was asleep, which helped me learn to talk again. I was so broken by the brain injury that I did not even understand what money was until I started healing and experiencing life. I marvel at just how amazing God truly is. I was so close to dying.

My hospital report said:

The current images do not extend completely through right pinna. The right pinna has been avulsed, and there is minimal soft tissue overlying the bone at the upper squamosal portion of the temporal bone. A portion of the cartilaginous portion of the external auditory canal is absent. There is focal soft tissue thickening along the cartilaginous external auditory canal, just external to the bony portion of the external auditory canal.

The right tympanic membrane is normal in appearance. The bony ossicles are normal in proportion. The course of the facial nerve is normal from the internal auditory canal to the stylomastoid foramen. Where the nerve exits the stylomastoid foramen is deep to the area of soft tissue avulsion.

Soft tissue windows reveal the retromandibular vein in its typical position in the right parotid gland, just posterior to the angle of the mandible. The expected course of the facial nerve appears to remain within the residual parotid tissue, although the most superficial portion of the parotid gland has been removed more superficially. A large band of thickened soft tissue is superficial to the right zygomatic arch and likely represent either graft material or scar material. The posterior half of the right zygomatic arch is absent. A calcification or vascular clip is to the fascia overlying the right temporal the right temporal muscle cephalad to the zygomatic arch. A small poster segment of the temporal muscle is absent.

I have learned humbleness and gratefulness firsthand! Though I sometimes make mistakes, I realize now that I must not tempt the Lord my God.

Contentment comes from the Heavenly Father. Now, I am not in a rush to do anything. I am precise about the tasks at hand, even though I have only one arm and one hand! My self-confidence has been restored by the Lord, and I have been blessed by the Lord to overcome the world; without this blessing, I would have continued to please Satan.

Thank you, Lord for blessing me to hear your voice!

You are my Lord, my God, my Savior.

Thanks be to thee!